CW01651042

Zigger Zagger

Lance Hattatt and James Sale

HODDER AND STOUGHTON
LONDON SYDNEY AUCKLAND TORONTO

Preface

Q is a series of English/Drama booklets for use with mixed-ability groups in the middle years of the secondary school. Standing independently of the text to which it relates, each booklet explores a well-known play through an informal but developing pattern of plot, character, theme, language and theatre.
Each section invites 'dipping-in'. Pupils will discover a wide range of lively and stimulating activities. These vary from discussion to writing, from recording to acting, and are designed to provide insight into a number of relevant and interesting topics.

Acknowledgments

The authors and publishers would like to thank the following for their kind permission to reproduce copyright texts in this volume: Penguin Books Ltd for various extracts from *Zigger Zagger* by Peter Terson; Martin Secker and Warburg Ltd and the Estate of the Late Sonia Brownell Orwell for an extract from *1984* by George Orwell; Martin Secker and Warburg for 'Suicides' from *New and Selected Poems* by J. C. Hall. We would be grateful for any information which may help us trace the copyright holder of 'Teddy Boy' by Tommy the Duffle.

The authors and publishers would also like to thank the following for permission to reproduce illustrations and photographs: Topham Picture Library (p. 22); *Private Eye* for 'Yobs' by Tony Husband (p. 28); and the National Youth Theatre (pp. 41 and 48).

ISBN 0 340 40163 X

First published 1987

Typeset by Rowland Phototypesetting Ltd, Bury St Edmunds, Suffolk.
Printed in Great Britain for Hodder and Stoughton Educational
a division of Hodder and Stoughton Ltd, Mill Road, Dunton Green, Sevenoaks, Kent by
St Edmundsbury Press Ltd, Bury St Edmunds, Suffolk.

Action Replay

Zigger Zagger – the Story of a Football Hooligan

Harry Philton is that hooligan. And it is his life the play follows.

Whether at home:

MOTHER

> They're lovely boys, aren't they? Lovely boys. Them footballers. (3)

At school:

HEADMASTER

> Is that all you do out there?
> Hang round the toilets and support the City? (7)

In court:

MAGISTRATE

> So remember, the next time you want to let off steam, do it in the football match, not outside it. (23)

Or in love,

SANDRA

> I'm happy at the City End, that's where my life is. (35)

It's football all the way. But it's not that simple. Harry has a problem: to take the advice of Les, his brother-in-law:

> At the end of a week, you want behind you a job well done, something learnt, a sense of achievement. With the weekend to rest in. Like Jesus said, the Sabbath.

or to go with Zigger, the leader of the football fans?

At the end of the week don't look behind you. Just look to tomorrow. Saturday, the big day, the big match, the lads trotting out the tunnel, the City roar.

To know more about Harry's problem, look carefully at the story chart.

GO OUT, LAD, INTO THE WORLD; IT ISN'T ALL FOOTBALL.
I WON'T COME BACK TO THIS DUMP.
LEAVING SCHOOL.
WHAT DID HE DO..?
THREW A BOTTLE AT A POLICEMAN, SIR.
CAUGHT OUT!
WOULD YOU LIKE TO TRY THE POLICE, YOU'VE GOT THE HEIGHT..?
I DON'T LIKE LAW AND ORDER.
DOWN THE JOB CENTRE.
SUPPORT THE TEAM, HARRY.
LEARN A TRADE, HARRY.
J.S. ENGINEERING
GETTING MORE ADVICE.
I WANT TO JOIN THE ARMED FORCES
YOU'RE NOT A.I., YOU'RE NOT A.I.
UNFIT.
YOU WANT SECURITY, HARRY.
YOU WANT A GOOD TIME, HARRY.
GETTING ADVICE.
I'LL LEARN A TRADE.
I'LL FIX YOU UP WITH A FIRM, THE MEN'LL LOOK AFTER YOU.
GOING STRAIGHT.
GREASE HIS PARTS.
INITIATION.
COME BACK TO THE STAND.
YOU'RE ONE OF THEM NOW, THEY'LL TAKE YOU TO THEM.
DECISION.

The story chart traces a major part of Harry's life to date.

At home his mother is less than interested in him. She gives him very little attention, reserves any love for her boyfriends, and doesn't seem too bothered about what happens to him. There is certainly not much evidence of a caring home. Indeed, in their own ways Les and Edna try to provide that.

In school Harry appears to fail. His teachers are not always sympathetic to his lack of success. Maybe he doesn't always try as hard as he could, but is there much motivation?

Job prospects are poor. His lack of qualifications doesn't help. Nor is he very good at presenting himself. For this he needs help – possibly professional. Harry's applications all seem to draw a blank. So much for Les's advice for security. In the circumstances, what Zigger says is not unattractive.

Life for Harry is hard: Sandra turns out to be fickle; Les's secure job has its unpleasant initiation ceremony; the future looks bleak. What kind of a future do you imagine it will be?

Perhaps it's not surprising Harry throws bottles at the City End, is it?

Whose fault is this?	His?
	Home?
	School?
	Society?

There is probably no one answer. In the end it must be a combination of all these things.

Who gives the best advice?	Les?
	Zigger?
What advice would you give?	Why?

LES

> You want security, Harry. A pension, a bit of insurance against old age and want.

ZIGGER

> You want a good time, Harry. All you want in old age is memories of the great old times.

Two very different pieces of advice! Make up a story in which a character takes one piece of advice and not the other. At the end of your story show how he/she regrets the choice made and wishes another decision had been taken.

'It's boring! There's nothing to do!' Have you ever thought something like this? Describe the things to do in your area. What would you like to happen? Suggest improvements that could be made.

'Leaving School'. Harry's in trouble on his last day – out of uniform, out of tune, out of order! Interview your parents. Find out how they spent their last day at school. Present this work as a tape, or cartoon, or improvisation, or playscript, or poem, or . . .

In groups, make up a drama sketch around one of these captions taken from the story chart:

Caught out!
Betrayed.
Decision.

Zigger Zagger is a play about modern life. What happens in it is familiar – football, booze, sex. Writing which deals with ordinary and everyday things is called **social realism**.

Features of Social Realism

1 Often concerns ordinary people.
2 Often deals with domestic and topical issues.
3 Often set in an urban environment.
4 Often uses slang and everyday language.

So, in **Zigger Zagger**:

1 Les and Edna are Mr and Mrs Average.
  Harry is one of today's youth.
2 Life at home figures throughout.
  Law and Order – a main problem of today.
3 The back of City End!
4 *You're a bastard referee.*
  The chairman is a puff.

Social realism may be seen in action:

(4) everyday language

(1) ordinary character

(2) a topical issue - pornography

FRANK

Hi, Harry, boy.

HARRY

You. Him. Uncle Frank. Dirty Frank. *Mother*, he's not a *newsagent*, he's an undercover agent. He's the agent for every *dirty magazine* that ever came out of the States. He's one dollar five cents Dan, the dirty newsagent man. We can't have him in the house.

FRANK

Now be fair, Harry. I also do 'Ideal Home' and 'Fur and Feather'. That's the many facets of me *business*.

(3) business - suggests urban environment

How many features of social realism can you find in these extracts?

THIRD STUDENT

This boy will be able to see the world, two years in Hong Kong's red light district. He'll come back a new man with a wealth of new experience.

HARRY

Git on. You university student fellers have nothing better to do but wave them silly bloody things.

You're the privileged class, you lot are, sitting up there getting educated. Getting stuffed full of knowledge at the expense of the workers. It's the working man does the graft and gets no wages, you student fellers get it all, don't you? All the good jobs. You take the plums. And you got nothing better to do but wave them things. A turn in the army wouldn't do you no harm.

FIRST STUDENT

Get the facts straight from a corpse.

SECOND STUDENT

When you come back you'll be able to scatter us with your hip throws.

THIRD STUDENT

With those muscles you'll be a wow in the Naafi.

FOURTH STUDENT

When you're captured they'll never be able to brainwash you, feller.

HARRY

Piss off. You educated gits. I'm going into the army. It's a man's life. It says so on the posters. You lot want put agin a brick wall and shot.

LAURENCE

Oh yes? Where do you shop?

ANGELA *(Speaking*
TONY *together)*

Sainsbury's.

LAURENCE

Ah, we usually go to the Co-op. I find they have a much wider range of goods there.

BEVERLY

Don't you find shopping boring, though, Ang?

ANGELA

Mmm.

BEVERLY

Oh, I do – I hate it. He takes me down in the car, and I get me wheely, Tone, and I whizz in, and I grab anything I can see, and I bung it in the wheely, he writes me a cheque, we bung it in the car, bring it home, and it's done for the week, d'you know what I mean?

LAURENCE

Beverly is not very organised: she doesn't believe in making shopping-lists. You have a car, do you?

TONY

Yeah.

ANGELA

Yes, an Escort.

LAURENCE

A yellow one?

ANGELA

That's it.

LAURENCE

Yes, I've seen it.

BEVERLY

Yeah, it's beautiful, actually.

ANGELA

Beverly was saying you only like Minis.

LAURENCE

No, not at all. I don't only like Minis – I like lots of other cars. But I find the Mini economical, efficient and reliable, and the most suited to my purposes. Of course, I change my car every year.

BEVERLY

Yeah, but what I say, Ang, is this: what is the point in changing your car if all you change is the colour?

LAURENCE

That's not all you change, Beverly; the design does alter. But then you're not a motorist, so of course you just don't understand these things.

BEVERLY

Yeah, okay. I know I failed my test three times.

Teddy Boy

(To Gloria, from Jail)

Wannit smashin', wannit smashin',
the dump where I hung out;
the Old Man use ter come 'ome cut
and knock me Mum about;
and last night's empties by the stairs
as up ter kip I goes,
and the tin trunk on the landin'
where I put me Teddy clothes.

Wannit smashin', wannit smashin',
the Palais and the Dive.
Remember when I done that bloke
fer askin' yer to jive?
And The Bug 'ouse every uvver night,
and fags and Dogs and beer.
I tell yer, I'm gonna Go The Lot
when I get out of 'ere.

TOMMY THE DUFFLE

Penalties!!

SOCCER MOB ON RAMPAGE

Court for City fans; violent scenes in town centre; mob breaks police cordon; passers-by terrified – two to General Hospital; Chief Inspector: fans surrounded; fleet of police vans.

77 ARRESTED AFTER NIGHT OF VIOLENCE

Cup-tie; 200 police; incidents in precinct; pubs closed – loss of business; arrests – night in cells; £150 theft – local food store; offenders – City fans.

FOOTBALL ROWDIES WARNED

Disturbance after match; rival gangs fight; five youths fined – bound over to keep peace; leader named – nineteen year old; frightened shoppers; manageress eye-witness.

Choose one of these headlines. As a newscaster, say on **News at Ten**, write the script of the story. Try taping it.

Read again Harry's monologue (scene 18). Write your own vivid, detailed description of crowds going to, at, and coming from a football match.

Football is not, of course, all negative. The majority of fans are, unlike Harry and Zigger, keen to support their team and interested in the sport. The problem is, how to overcome the bad publicity?

Much can be done to persuade people that football is still a game for the family. Try these ideas. Can you think of any more?

Football For the Family

Design a poster to encourage people of all ages to support their local club.

Write an introduction to your club programme, pointing out all the advantages of membership.

Write to the editor of your local newspaper in support of football and its followers.

Good publicity is not enough in itself. People like Harry and Zigger cannot be ignored. Everyone has a part to play – home, school, police. It is difficult to decide what is for the best.

'There is too much leniency. There should be more severe punishment.'

What ideas have you for preventing football hooliganism? How would you enforce your ideas?

Punks v Pinstripes

I couldn't half fancy them footballers.

He's a hard case.

But is there any purpose in life, see?

You can always look to me for counsel.

Les. You're wonderful.

Two of the portraits need to be completed. How would you picture Mrs Philton and Edna? These extracts should help you to decide:

MRS PHILTON *(to Harry)*

Can you not become a footballer? Then introduce me to your friends. Some big chunky goal-getting centre forward.

MRS PHILTON

I've got to get to the bottom of it, Harry. I promised the Director. Nice man that. I was surprised, gold chain, medal and smelled beautiful; we got on like a house on fire.

EDNA

That's right, Harry. Les finds it *(Reader's Digest)* a fount of knowledge.

EDNA *(playing Scrabble)*

You're so daring with it, Les. I'd have been worried stiff with an X in my hand.

Clearly Mrs Philton fancies any man, whilst poor Edna has no personality of her own at all. She simply idolises her husband, Les.

Appearances can be deceptive. Although they give clues as to what people are like, they do not tell us accurately. Why is this?

To form opinions about people, we need to know more than what they look like. To understand *character*, we need to:

see what people say
see what people do
see what others say about them

Take Harry, for example. He's a bit mixed up. Half of him wants to be like Zigger, a rebel. The other half, to conform, like Les. Look at some of the things he says:

I'm not going to no psychiatrist. I'm not daft. (11)

I would like a job with adventure. Like on the telly. (12)

I'm for the lads at the City End who don't give a damn. (17)

I'm getting on now, mother. Soon be settling, mebbe getting engaged. (31)

I've got a lot to learn, haven't I? (31)

Or some of the things said about him:

He's just like the rest of them. Stupid. (2)

Never short of money, never short of money. (5)

Les, you're doing a lot for that boy. He looks up to you like a father. (32)

He's too serious. (35)

Or the things he does:

HARRY
- chews pencils
- pinches rubbers
- delivers papers
- supports City
- throws bottles
- dates Sandra
- hurls insults
- makes lamps

Like most people, Harry has his good and bad points – the positive and negative sides of his character. Decide what is good about him, what is bad, and complete the character box. Some words have been put in to start you off.

Negative	Positive
Violent	Reliable
Aggressive	

Which of these situations is likely to bring out the positive side of his character, which the negative? Think carefully. Can you say why?

Harry's school
Les and Edna's house
At the match
The Youth Careers Office
The Magistrates' Court
The Supporters' Club Dance

It is easy when looking at character to think in terms of good and bad. But people generally, and Harry is no exception, are much more complex.

Nearly everyone is a mixture. Les is well meaning with his advice, 'Learn a trade, Harry', but is a bit of a bore:

> Very interesting programme on the telly. We've switched it off. I think when you've got visitors you should switch off. We both think that, don't we, Edna? I know Edna does. Switch off, television ruins conversation.

Mrs Philton cares for Harry:

> Tell your mum.

But cares more for herself:

> I'm all upset. Me nerves is shattered.

Consider either Les or Mrs Philton. List good and bad points – *characteristics.* Arrange your words in a character box similar to Harry's. Some characteristics may appear neither good nor bad – neutral. List these separately. Here are some to start you off:

cautious
methodical
carefree

What about yourself? Have you ever seriously thought what kind of a person you are? What do people like about you? What may they dislike? Make up your own character box!

Harry's not the only one unsure of himself. Edna, Les, and Sandra are none too happy.

Edna's a bit lonely. She writes to Radio 2. It seems all the romance has gone out of her life.

Les's hands have become very rough (all that pipe-work) and he won't go to a manicurist. He's not keen on going out for a bit of a drink either. Harry is Les's worry. Young boy going to waste. Won't get himself a trade. Hangs around with the football crowd and that flighty girl, Sandra.

Sandra? Well, she's sort of two-timing. Stringing Harry along but really in love with Vincent. Trouble is, he's just gone to the top of the transfer list.

They're all in need of some sound, practical advice. Why not give it to them?

Either complete Edna's letter (and Patsy's reply) or write similar letters from (a) Les or (b) Sandra.

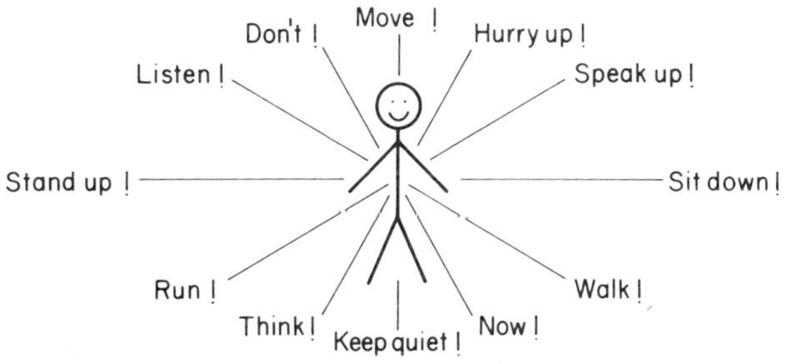

Are these some of the things you're told to do – or not to do? Who by? Usually parents, teachers, people in authority – those who have a legal power or right over you.

Many of the adults in **Zigger Zagger** are in positions of authority – the Headmaster; Harry's teacher; Mrs Philton; Chairman of the Football Club; Youth Careers Officer; Recruiting Sergeant; Magistrate; Youth Club Leader. If you think carefully, there are probably others.

The way in which authority is used will depend on strength of character. By looking at authority figures in action, we can learn about them as people. In the case of the Headmaster, his authority is fairly considerable. Among other things he must:

1 Provide a framework for education.
2 Ensure the smooth running of the school.
3 Set standards of work, discipline, conduct, etc.
4 Deal with problems arising in school.

To do this, he must exercise his authority over the staff, the pupils, and even the parents. In fact, throughout the school.

How successful is he?

HEADMASTER

> I'm Harry Philton's Headmaster. He's just like the rest of them. Stupid. If he'd left school when he was twelve, he'd have left knowing as much as he does now. Besides, he chews the ends off the pencils.

He is quick to call Harry stupid. Hardly very fair. He probably doesn't even know him as a person. And if Harry is stupid, why is this? It may be he hasn't had the kind of schooling best suited to his needs. After all, if Harry would have been just as well off leaving school at twelve, something must be wrong.

In assembly, the 'louts' at the back disrupt. The Headmaster's response is predictable. He speaks out against

> The people who have got nothing out of school life, and put nothing in. The people who think all the world's a football pitch.

going on to say that

> For the rest of us there are more things in life than football.

It is all very well saying there are more things in life, but he makes no attempt to demonstrate what these things are.

Even as Harry leaves, the Headmaster is acknowledging what is happening in the toilets. He appears unable, or unwilling, to stop the acts of vandalism.

HEADMASTER

> There's always one who is too weak to find his own way. Has to follow the mob. Quiet as a mouse at heart, but stick him on the football terrace and he becomes like the rest. They're at the toilets now. Every leaving time is the same. They stick toilet rolls down the lavatory, bend the new aluminium coatpegs (if you knew how much the taxpayer pays in coatpeg replacements). They crack the basins, bust the locks, vandalism. What can I do? They've left. Is that all you can do out there? Hang around the toilets and support the City?

Not a very good record it would seem. What kind of a man emerges? What can be said about his character? How many of these characteristics would you agree with?

> unsympathetic; unthinking; insensitive; narrow; prejudiced; pompous; self-opinionated; lacking resolve; inadequate; imperceptive; weak; cowardly; disciplinarian; Christian; concerned; wise; helpful; forgiving.

Discuss these qualities. Add to them.

Now try to find out what kind of a person the Youth Careers Officer is. It may be helpful to look back at scene 12.

1 What kind of authority does he have?
2 Who is his authority over?
3 How successful is he?
4 What characteristics emerge?

Can you do the same for some of the others?

All the people in authority mentioned come into contact with Harry at some time or another. Harry is a problem person. The school decides on a 'Case Conference' to discuss his present progress and his future.

With the Headmaster taking the chair, Harry's teacher, the Youth Careers Officer and Mrs Philton are invited to attend. Additionally, it is felt useful to have the Youth Club Leader and the local Magistrate present.

Discuss each of the characters in turn, deciding how each will react in this situation. Now act out the 'Case Conference'. Afterwards, write a report on what has taken place and what has been decided. Do this from each character's viewpoint. So, the Headmaster will write his account, Mrs Philton hers, and so on.

The 'Case Conference' gives a good idea of how some of the adults view Harry. But what is the real Harry? How will his life work out?

From what *you* know of Harry, build up his life story in the form of a biography. The story chart should suggest ideas.

Harry Philton

You know he is about 16. Where was he born? When?
(Draw out his birth certificate.)
Who is his father? Grandparents? What do they do?
(Find or draw pictures of them. Construct a family tree.)
Where does he live?
(Draw a sketch map of his city or town.)
Which schools has he been to?
(Include a school report.)
On holiday with Mum and 'Uncle' Brian.
(Keep a record of the holiday – include snapshots.)

Having got going, it's up to you to carry on. Fill the biography with as many lively and original ideas as you can. See how well you can present your work.

Born victims, these kids. Born losers. They have seen through it all, they have given up. Apathetic, then aggressive.

(*The Times*, 8 October, 1985)

Discuss this comment. How true is it of Harry and Zigger?

Foul Play

From the stands of Leeds United
To the back of White Hart Lane
We will wave the City banners
Till the City's top again.
We will beat the Spurs and Gunners,
The Hammers and the Kop,
We will spur them on to victory
Till City are the top.

Great! But is this all there is to **Zigger Zagger**? Obviously not. To find out the ideas Peter Terson is really exploring, try this simple quiz. Just match the statements in A to the words in B.

	A	**B**
1	I think you're everything	authority
2	Lawful folk being terrorised	futility
3	I'll fix you up with a firm	violence
4	We've hung around the toilets our school life	work
5	Away from here. This is Education Committee private property now you've left	love

Answers

1 = 5
2 = 3
3 = 4
4 = 2
5 = 1

It's easy now to see what Peter Terson is doing. Authority, futility, love, violence and work are all themes central to the play. Of these, futility and violence are both very much a part of everyday life. Sadly, violence is all too easily recognisable and understood. Futility, perhaps, is less so.

Futility – uselessness, without purpose, incapable of producing any result.

How true is this of **Zigger Zagger**? Well, Zigger himself leads a pretty aimless life. On the terraces, yes, he's fully in command:

> I lead them. The whole living block of them. A dense mass of red and white. I'm lifted onto their shoulders and I start the cry: Zigger Zagger, Zigger Zagger.

But to what purpose? None. Does he question what he is doing? Unlikely.

Harry, influenced as he is by Zigger, is not quite the same. Yes, much of what he does appears senseless but, unlike Zigger, he does occasionally wonder where it's all leading:

> There sometimes seems nothing to live for, you know. Nothing. Jobs, nor life, nor nothing.

Remembering his dead-end school leading to his dead-end job, it's not surprising that he sees life as futile and behaves accordingly. Perhaps it's all a matter of cause and effect.

Harry feels he fails at school, so he expresses his frustration with acts of vandalism – toilet rolls down the lavatory, bending coatpegs, cracking basins, busting locks.

When he fails to join the army, he goes on the rampage with 'the lads at the City End who don't give a damn'.

When he fails to fit into the youth club, he goes wild on the buses.

In failing to keep Sandra, he loses faith even in football – 'the football terrace is the fool's church pew'.

What does it all add up to? Not a lot. It's all fairly pointless. Even at the end of the play, Harry remains much as he was. There is little to suggest that his future life will prove any less futile.

What of the other characters? Are their lives any more purposeful? It's not easy to decide and depends how *you* view things. Take Les and Edna, for instance. Is there any point to the things Les does?

> I like to take my home, and put my own stamp on it; if there's a bare wall, I paper it; a door, paint it; a piece of wood, stain it; a picture, frame it; a light

bulb, shade it; a hole, polyfil it; a table top, vinyl cover it; a piece of foam rubber, cushion it; a delightful moment, photograph it; a piece of music, record it; And the result?

Well, what is the result? Is there one?

Or what about Sandra? She looks for a life of 'excitement, cigarette smoke, wind over the pitch, the smell of the crowd, the knee-deep litter'.

Do you see a purpose here?

Consider your own life. How purposeful is it? Think of all the kinds of things you do, both at home and at school. List them under the heading FUTILE and PURPOSEFUL. Be prepared to give reasons for your decisions. We have done some to start you off. You may not, of course, agree with our choices!

Futile	**Purposeful**
smoking	paper round
swearing	homework
fighting	walking the dog
	doing this!

Many of life's activities can appear either futile or purposeful. So much depends on attitudes and circumstances.

Divide into small groups. Think about these situations:

On the Terraces
At the Youth Club
Street Corner
Downtown Disco

Improvise them in *two* ways: (a) to show futility;
(b) positively.

Whatever we think of Zigger and Sandra, or Les and Edna, *they* think they have a purpose in life. And Harry, well, he *wants* a purpose. The play, **Zigger Zagger**, charts Harry's search for a purpose – for something in life that isn't futile.

But supposing he couldn't find any purpose at all. Supposing he gave up trying. What then? SUICIDE?

Suicides

Reading the evening papers we meet them,
Those anonymous names:
She who turned the gas on her sorrow,
He whom the Thames
Left one night more derelict on its shore
Than a child at the convent door.

Little we knew them, these who in their lives
Rated no column.
And even now only between the lines
May we glimpse the solemn
Dilemmas that drove them thither and guess
Something of their last loneliness.

What of this girl? Surely her beauty might
Have confounded the shades?
Or was it beauty itself that led her
Into the glades
Of darkness, where, by love's fever oppressed,
She sought to be dispossessed?

And what of him they found in the chilly dawn
With the tide in his hair?
They say in drowning a man unravels all
His history there
In a fleeting moment, before he falls away
On eternal silence. So he may

Have found at last in some long-sought, half-forgotten
Memory a mirror
Reflecting his first true self, distorted since
By childhood terror.
Oh then perhaps – the pattern revealed – too late
He saw his meaningless fate . . .

We cannot know. For even the notes they left
In their desolate rooms
Can tell us little but that our restless souls
To unknown dooms
Move on, while still, deep in each human face,
We seek the signature of grace.

Tragic their deaths, more tragic the aching thought
That had we been there
We might have laid our hands on their hands and begged
'Do not despair!

For here, even here in this living touch, this breath,
May be the solace you seek in death.'

J. C. HALL

What sort of people are these 'suicides'? It says they had 'anonymous names', that their lives 'Rated no column', and that we can 'guess/Something of their last loneliness'. How does this compare with Harry Philton's situation?

Although the poem deals with despair and futility, it does not end on this note. It suggests that 'this living touch, this breath' might be enough to prevent suicide. Again, how true is this of Harry Philton – who is the 'living touch' for him?

Imagine that Les and Edna are killed in a car-accident just after Les promises to get Harry fixed up with the lads (37). How would this affect the ending of the play?

Discuss in groups, improvise, and write out the new last scenes. Would Harry leave a suicide note? to his mother? Sandra? Zigger?

From **Zigger Zagger** and 'Suicides' it is clear that human contact is very important in our lives. Without love and acceptance, Harry and the suicides are unable to cope. They feel so unimportant.

The play **Zigger Zagger** shows the different stages in the life of Harry: from being a school vandal to being a football hooligan to becoming an apprentice. The poem 'Suicides' is much shorter. It ignores all the details of his and her sad story – it tries to discuss the basic reason why they killed themselves.

Try to write your poem about Harry. Avoid including all the details we know about from the play. Concentrate on the decision he had to make and the reason(s) for his eventual choice. A title might be 'Do not despair!'

Suicides centres on two people, a girl and a man, both driven to the desperate lengths of taking their own lives. Use the ideas of the poem for your own work:

1 For either the girl or the man, write a personal diary to cover the days leading up to the moment of suicide.
2 'They say in drowning a man unravels all his history.' Write the life story of the man.
3 Discuss in small groups the reasons which might have led to the suicides described in the poem. Act out a scene in which either the girl or the man seeks help from a friend.

On a lighter note, futility is portrayed in Yobs – a cartoon in the magazine **Private Eye** (see page 28).

The senseless act of vandalism needs no explanation. Try creating a similar cartoon of your own.

Violence – roughness, force

Study these two pictures carefully.

Both show potentially violent scenes. But are they the same? No. The violence in each is very different. The two boxers are in a controlled situation. The football crowd, on the other hand, represents uncontrolled violence. Of the two, this is so much more frightening. And this is the kind of violence so often found in **Zigger Zagger**

Zigger Zagger *is* concerned with violence. Violence which takes three distinct forms: *physical*, *mental*, and *verbal*.

Of these, physical hurts the body
mental hurts the mind
verbal accompanies both.

Applied to the play we see,
Blues and Reds fighting
Zigger and Harry inflicting racist comments
Obscene, unacceptable language.

Physical violence is, of course, the most easily recognized form. What prompts this kind of behaviour remains uncertain. What is clear, though, is the widespread distress and suffering it can cause.

Harry hurls a bottle at a policeman. The policeman is hit. Is this is the end of the matter? No. Look at all the others who become involved.

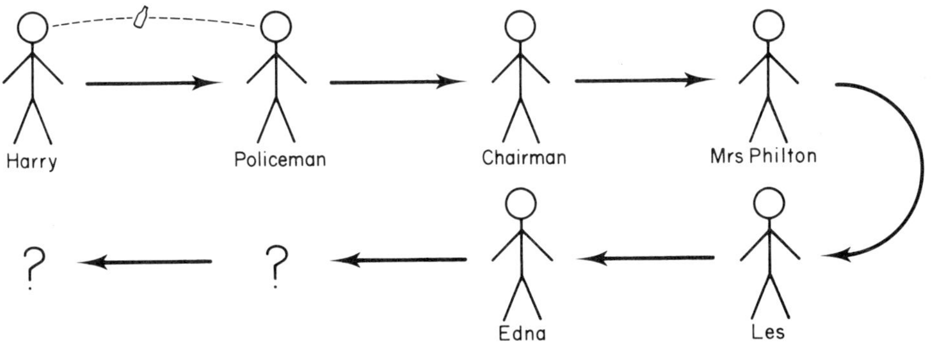

Can you say in what ways each is affected? Can you think of any other people who could become involved?

Bottle throwing, toilet roll throwing, going about the country to away matches, smashing up cafes, bringing back souvenirs . . .

A further example of Zigger and Harry's handiwork. How many different people are likely to be affected here?

Just as painful is mental violence – violence which disturbs and threatens not the body but the mind.

In **Zigger Zagger** those who suffer are members of society. Who do you feel is intimidated most? Can you say why? Maybe Harry suffers more than we think. After all, he hasn't achieved much at school; he's constantly torn between Zigger and Les; the mental pressure is quite considerable. Little wonder he has a go at his 'Uncle' Brian!

George Orwell's **1984** portrays a horrifying picture of a Britain where mental cruelty is used as a device to ensure conformity. In this extract Winston Smith faces his tormentor, O'Brien, an Inner Party member. O'Brien makes it clear: this is not just physical violence.

He had moved a little to one side, so that Winston had a better view of the thing on the table. It was an oblong wire cage with a handle on top for carrying it by. Fixed to the front of it was something that looked like a fencing mask, with the concave side outwards. Although it was three or four metres away from him, he could see that the cage was divided lengthways into two compartments, and that there was some kind of creature in each. They were rats.

'In your case,' said O'Brien, 'the worst thing in the world happens to be rats.'

A sort of premonitory tremor, a fear of he was not certain what, had passed through Winston as soon as he caught his first glimpse of the cage. But at this moment the meaning of the mask-like attachment in front of it suddenly sank into him. His bowels seemed to turn to water.

'You can't do that!' he cried out in a high cracked voice. 'You couldn't, you couldn't! It's impossible.'

'The rat,' said O'Brien, still addressing his invisible audience, 'although a rodent, is carnivorous. You are aware of that. You will have heard of the things that happen in the poor quarters of this town. In some streets a woman dare not leave her baby alone in the house, even for five minutes. The rats are certain to attack it. Within quite a small time they will strip it to the bones. They also attack sick or dying people. They show astonishing intelligence in knowing when a human being is helpless.'

'I have pressed the first lever,' said O'Brien. 'You understand the construction of this cage. The mask will fit over your head, leaving no exit. When I press this other lever, the door of the cage will slide up. These starving brutes will shoot out of it like bullets. Have you ever seen a rat leap through the air? They will leap on to your face and bore straight into it. Sometimes they attack the eyes first. Sometimes they burrow through the cheeks and devour the tongue.'

The mask was closing on his face. The wire brushed his cheek. And then – no, it was not relief, only hope, a tiny fragment of hope. Too late, perhaps too late. But he had suddenly understood that in the whole world there was just *one* person to whom he could transfer his punishment – *one* body that he could thrust between himself and the rats. And he was shouting frantically, over and over.

'Do it to Julia! Do it to Julia! Not me! Julia! I don't care what you do to her. Tear her face off, strip her to the bones. Not me! Julia! Not me!'

He was falling backwards, into enormous depths, away from the rats. He was still strapped in the chair, but he had fallen through the floor, through the walls of the building, through the earth, through the oceans, through the atmosphere, into outer space, into the gulfs between the stars – always away, away, away from the rats. He was light-years distant, but O'Brien was still standing at his side. There was still the cold touch of a wire against his cheek. But through the darkness that enveloped him he heard another metallic click, and knew that the cage door had clicked shut and not open.

This may seem a long way from Harry Philton's situation. But is it? What similarities can you pick out between Harry and Winston's situation?

Who wants Harry to conform? List them. What pressures do they apply? For example:

The Headmaster	*Pressures*	
	reason (mental) –	'You were a good lad when you were eleven – where's it gone?'
	insult (verbal) –	'one by one you're not so brave'
	law (physical) –	'Away, or I'll call the police'

Who else?

O'Brien's method works on the idea of fear. In the end, the individual can be made to conform because their weakness is found. Is this true? Could Zigger Zagger be *made* to conform? Remember, we saw earlier how love and acceptance saved Harry from despair and futility.

Write a story describing the confrontation between O'Brien and Zigger. Make sure you include 'the worst thing in the world' for Zigger.

What makes O'Brien's form of violence so effective? How convincing is Winston's phobia of rats? Do you have a fear of something without reason? Talk about it.

Decide the events immediately prior to Winston's interrogation. Dramatise the whole scene.

In small groups, construct a short radio play to describe the arrest of Julia. Tape your work. Include sound effects.

> Sticks and stones may break my bones
> But words can never hurt me.

True. But verbal abuse can be very upsetting. Both Zigger and Harry use such abuse regularly. Furthermore, most of the songs are intended to threaten with the language they use. Can you say why certain words carry so much more force when used in song?

One obvious consequence of all violence is **alienation**.

People committing violent acts are increasingly alienated. They appear friendless. Society turns away from them. All too often they end up alone. Sometimes in prison. Such could be the fate of Zigger.

Write a letter to Harry from a repentant Zigger describing life behind bars.

Script the dialogue between Zigger and his girlfriend, Glenice, on visiting day.

Following Zigger's application for remission, write the prison governor's report on him.

Parole Board. Act out Zigger's appearance before this important committee.

To develop the two themes of **futility** and **violence** further, try these activities:

'Be a free man. Go and drift.' Zigger's advice. Describe what happens when Harry does just this.

> I've fallen in love with my idol.
> Vincent! Vincent! Vincent! Vincent!

Devise and act out an extra scene for the play in which Sandra's parents try to persuade her to give up Vincent.

This old person has just returned home from shopping. She is about to become a victim of a break-in. Inside, her house is wrecked, her savings stolen.

1. Write about her thoughts and feelings both now *and* once indoors.
2. Make up the statement which she makes to the police.
3. Dramatise the events which follow her entry into the house.

In Harper Lee's **To Kill a Mockingbird**, thirteen-year-old Jem is driven to cutting the heads off Mrs Dubose's prize camellias because of her wounding and insulting remarks.

> He did not begin to calm down until he had cut the tops off every camellia bush Mrs Dubose owned, until the ground was littered with green buds and leaves. (Chapter 11)

1. Write the letter Mrs Dubose might have written to Jem's father, Atticus Finch, complaining of his son's behaviour.
2. Describe a time when you were provoked to do some wilful action. Indicate the outcome.

3 Use 'Revenge' as a title for improvisations. Create three short sketches dealing with 'Revenge' as a response to our three forms of violence: mental, physical, and verbal. Be careful to rank the level of 'revenge' with the mode of violence. The last sketch should show the most drastic form of revenge – but which form of violence will this be in response to? You must decide which is the worst form.

Finally, a graffiti wall. Put away the spray paint can and turn your hand to some clever, witty slogans. Can you match any of these?

Attacking Tactic

Language in **Zigger-Zagger** is down-to-earth and ordinary. The characters in the play come from backgrounds that we can readily understand. If we look at the vocabulary used, we find there are no 'difficult' words. Often characters swear. We are familiar with the way they express themselves. But this does not mean their language is just 'simple'.

Zigger Zagger is a play which shows extreme emotional states. What sort of emotions? You might like to consider the full range, but one particular type is very important: anger, hostility, resentment – or just plain aggression. Zigger, Sandra and Harry are fighting a battle against society. And society is fighting against them. Later, Zigger and Sandra turn against Harry, who wants to 'integrate'.

Some of the battles are fought with bottles. Mostly the fighting is through words. We saw this when we discussed verbal violence: mocking chants, obscene language, and direct insults. The language must have an 'attacking' edge.

One 'Attacking Tactic' which is extremely powerful in **Zigger Zagger** is **irony**.

Chants, obscenity, insults are direct ways of attacking.

'the ref's a bastard' = a chant + an obscenity + an insult!

Irony is indirect, and more subtle. Irony attacks the characters and shows us their weaknesses.

To understand what irony is, we need first to look at the more well-known, but similar, figure of speech, **sarcasm**.

> A landlocked little paradise with plastic palm trees and a muralette of Tahiti on the wall.

Zigger describes what he sees – and is disgusted by it. He mocks Les and Edna's house. His tone is sarcastic and his words show sarcasm. Sarcasm tells the truth, but does it in a way that shows dislike and disgust in order to hurt.

What other examples can you find in **Zigger Zagger**? Nobody likes to be on the receiving end of sarcasm. Discuss examples in your life: have you used it against someone, or been on the receiving end? What is the effect of sarcasm? Does it help relationships?

Irony is a way of speaking in which the opposite is always meant! Unlike sarcasm, where the truth is stated but mocked, irony can involve lies.

Stanley invites Harry and Zigger into the Youth Club. Zigger says: 'Not now, feller, actually. Got another engagement'. Has he another engagement? No! He is using irony – sounding polite to mock Stanley. He does not want to go inside with him. We – and perhaps Stanley (depending on how the words are said) – understand Zigger to mean the opposite of what he says.

The words he speaks mean 'Sorry, I'd like to enter but unfortunately I can't', but he really means 'Get lost'.

But just as sarcasm can tell the truth, so can irony. It can be difficult to distinguish between them.

What is irony?

Harry tells the Youth Careers Officer what qualifications he has: only a Bronze Medallion for Life Saving and Tenderfoot in the Cubs. The Youth Careers Officer says: 'So, all we need is a job in a forest, by a lake, saving lives.' Is he being helpful? Is he trying to find that sort of job for Harry? No! Again, he is mocking – through irony he is trying to make Harry feel his inadequacies.

Now look at the following, and explain why they are ironical.

First Student (scene 15) to Harry: 'The army offers you a chance to learn a trade.'

Third Student (scene 15) to Harry: 'This boy will be able to see the world, two years in Hong Kong's red light district. He'll come back a new man with a wealth of new experience.'

Fourth Student (scene 15) to Harry: 'When you're captured they'll never be able to brainwash you, feller.'

Harry (scene 9) to the Policeman: 'No I just got wet eyes. They water easily in the wind.'

Zigger (scene 31) to the audience: 'Les's is the perfect British home, Les is the perfect British worker. Les is the perfect British citizen as outlined in the latest booklet of the Central Office of Information.'

What other examples can you find? Discuss. Draw a cartoon to illustrate the irony.

Sometimes the irony is not through what is spoken, but what happens.

Events – the **situation** – seems to contradict what has gone before.

Harry wants to fight	irony →	rejected by the army
Zigger says Youth Clubs are full of ponces	irony →	the ju-jitsu 'ponce' throws Zigger out
Les persuades Harry to leave violence	irony →	Apprentices' ceremony of acceptance is violent

Irony helps us to avoid taking the characters at 'face-value'. Irony helps us see how ridiculous some attitudes are.

Now discuss the ironies in:

1. Harry entering a church to look for meaning in life . . .
2. The Chairman giving Harry a 'shock' . . .
3. Vincent is the hero of the crowd but . . .
4. Harry gets Sandra to like football . . .
5. Mrs Philton expresses a deep interest in football . . .

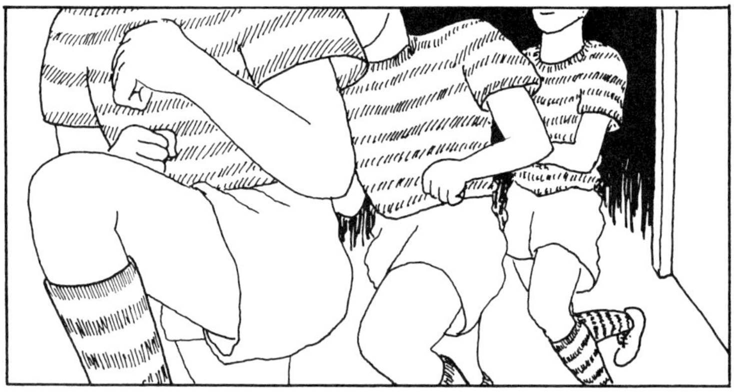

Ironies are not only common in **Zigger Zagger** but also in life. Can you think of any incidents where what was done contradicted what was said? Discuss.

Write an essay, called 'The Irony', about such an incident.

Chants, Moves, and the Big Match

Chants

We said at the beginning that **Zigger Zagger** was a play of social realism. It deals with modern issues in a believable way. For example, **Zigger Zagger** deals with football hooliganism and the problems of one-parent families.

At the same time **Zigger Zagger** is not completely realistic. Scene 6 begins with Zigger as the **narrator**. All of scene 18, except the last part, is Harry's **monologue**. And throughout the play there are constant **chants** and **choruses**. What do these mean, and why are they there?

Who is the central character in **Zigger Zagger**? Strange as it may seem, it is not Zigger; it is Harry. Our interest in Harry comes from knowing that he is torn in two opposite directions:

ZIGGER to join HARRY to join LES

Zigger despises Les: 'What you want to learn a trade? Be a free man.'

Les pities Zigger: 'You don't want to come like him, Harry. Not you.'

Having a **narrator**
a **monologue**
and **chants/choruses**
helps us see **dramatically** the **mental** struggle going on.

Harry Philton is not too bright ('When he was eleven he could add fractions but not do decimals. Now he's fifteen he's doing decimals but he's forgotten fractions.') He can't explain the problems facing him. But we can see the problem when Zigger describes Les and Edna's house: Les and Edna don't seem *real*.

We see the interior first. It looks 'nice'? Then Zigger steps out to describe it – he **narrates** its 'story' – doesn't it seem very different?

'A do-it-yourself house . . . pre-packed nails . . . pre-packed coat-hangers . . . a do-it-yourself husband . . .'

Now look at scenes 35 and 36. Harry is near a church. Zigger mocks the messages displayed outside the Church. Imagine a set for the interior of the church – Zigger steps on as the narrator. Write his short speech, picking out the things he would mock and disapprove of.

There are two sides to every story as **Zigger Zagger** makes clear. Look at The Supporters' Club Dance. Now imagine Les viewing the spectacle. If he were narrating, what would he say about what he saw?

Write his short speech.

When you have done both, act out the role of the narrator using your own script.

Narrating need not be negative. Sometimes it records the facts. Look at Zigger later. He tells how Sandra became 'the great female fan'. But his story is full of admiration:

> 'The three o'clock kick-off was her kiss of life'
> ''Tis a moment some remember yet'
> 'Sandra was there as he thundered down' (scene 34)

Zigger makes the event sound exciting and glamorous.

Harry seems to think the army is 'a man's life'. Form into groups of about eight. Improvise a scene in which Harry, as a new recruit, is watching army manoeuvres. Harry 'narrates' what he sees.

A **monologue** is one person speaking on the stage. Usually, this tells us what they think and feel. Harry's monologue is like Zigger's **narration**: they are both excited by events at the match.

Ordinary conversation wouldn't convey the *personal* sense of excitement. So Peter Terson gets the characters to say what they see and feel.

The big match excites Zigger, Harry, and Sandra. What big occasions have excited you?

Choose your own, or one of the following, and write and dramatically present a monologue on it:

A sporting event
Christmas shopping in the city
A funfair
A circus
A pop or rock music concert
A holiday camp

The full excitement of a big event cannot be stated by one character. Football is about crowds – cheering and booing. In a football match right and wrong are simple: right is your team, and wrong is the opponents'.

This is why the **chants** and **choruses** in **Zigger Zagger** are so important:

The **chants** help create the exciting atmosphere of the big match.
The **choruses** help give us the other side of the story.

On the original stage version, the set was made to look like a stadium. The players, when they had finished on stage, sat in the 'terraces'!

To see how exciting this can be, try it: take Scene 26. Form a semi-circle. Choose a Harry, a Sandra, and Zigger to stand some space in front. Then let rip: Harry says, 'I can't hear you!'

Now look at the following scenes.

Scene 7
The Headteacher gives his views
Class Chorus give theirs

Scene 9
The Chairman gives his views
Class Chorus give theirs

Scene 12
Youth Careers Officer gives his views
Class Chorus gives theirs

The Chorus gives a response:

1	*the Headteacher* 'Go on. Away, or I'll call the police.'	*Chorus* 'We shall not, we shall not be moved.'
2	*the Chairman* 'Go on, hurry along. Before I change my mind.'	*Chorus* 'The Chairman is a puff.'
3	*the Youth Careers Officer* 'Shouting for jobs, shouting for jobs.'	*Chorus* 'I'm forever blowing bubbles.'

1 The Headmaster tells them to move: the football supporters challenge this.

2 The Chairman fails to discipline Harry: the football supporters call him weak and effeminate, 'a puff'.

3 The Youth Careers Officer talks of jobs: the football supporters think his ideas are dreams.

Find three more examples of the Chorus commenting on some character's words. What affect does the Chorus have?

The Chants and Choruses create excitement, challenge opinions and authority. Often the tune is a well-known song or hymn. But the words are changed.

The new words usually poke fun at the old ideas, or they 'worship' the new 'idol' – football, Vincent, City, etc.

The most dramatic example is probably during the final school assembly. The change happens halfway through the hymn!

Earlier, the Class has sung a 'Farewell Hymn'. This has all the words the Headmaster wants. But the Headmaster can no longer control his pupils. During hymn 397, 'Guide me, O thou great Redeemer', the words change:

> 'City, City, City, City,
> We'll support you evermore'

The Headmaster loses control – the pupils now follow a new leader: the City Football team.

The Headmaster tries to reason with the pupils. His pupils find the chants/songs far more appealing. Which appeal to you most, reasons or songs? Discuss their influence on your life.

Imagine the pupils all supported a pop singer. Change the words of hymn 397 to show this. Perform it.

Discuss well-known songs and hymns and attempt to write new football words. Then perform them.

Moves

The position of characters on stage is important. It should:

1. Help the audience find the centre of attention;
2. provide a clear view (the **sightlines**) of the action;
3. enable the players to move freely.

Positioning the movements of the players on stage – from their entrance to their exit – is called **blocking**. Many directors **block** as the first step in their rehearsals. Areas of the stage are normally divided like this:

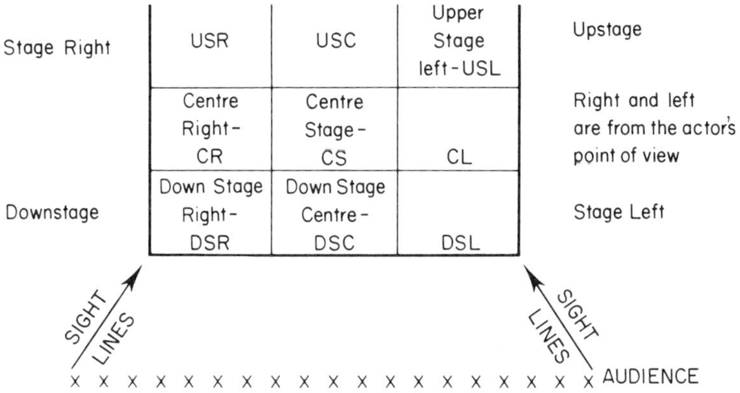

Complete the descriptions of the remaining abbreviations. Abbreviations like this are useful. We can write: Z enters USR × CS = Zigger Zagger enters Upper Stage Right and crosses to centre stage. A diagram of this movement would look like this:

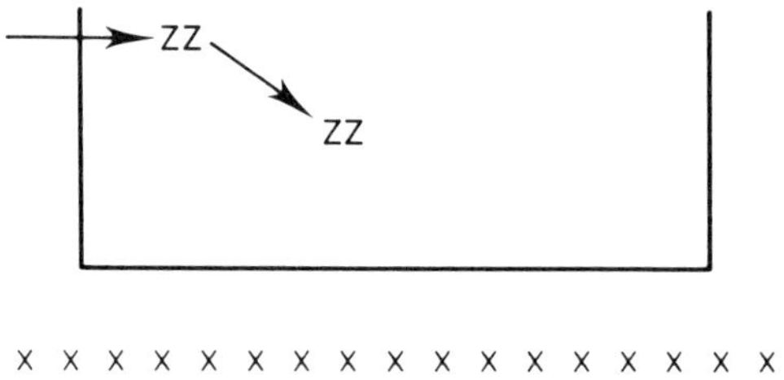

Now turn to Scene 35. We see Zigger enters to meet Sandra and Harry. They are already on stage. Where?

Imagine this was the arrangement:

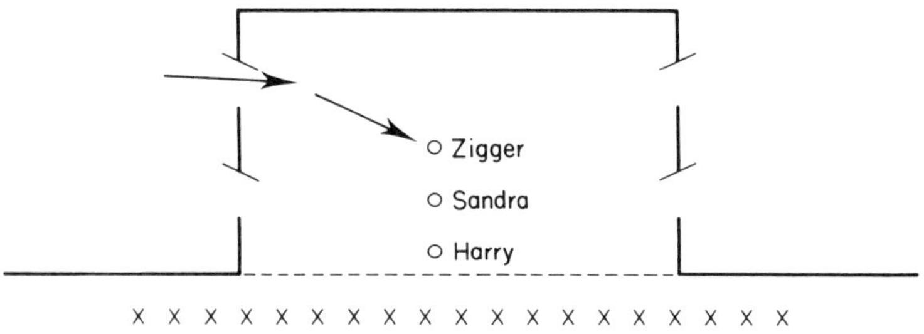

What special problems for the audience does this present? What problems for the players?

If we look at the scene closely, we can see that Harry and Sandra are having a tiff:

1 Will they be near or apart on stage?

Zigger comes on stage, but whose side of the argument does he take?

2 Will he be nearer Sandra or Harry?

Sandra leaves without Harry. Zigger and Harry disagree.

3 Will Harry, Sandra, Zigger use the same exit?

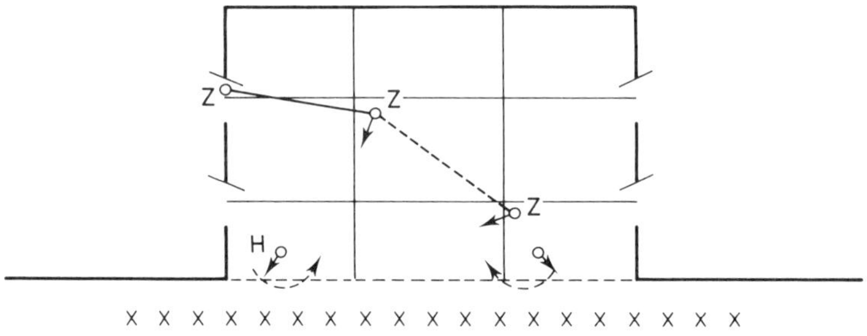

	Sandra/DSL	**Harry/DSR**
	facing away from each other	
Z:	What's wrong with the young stuff then, eh?	**Z enters USR × CS**
S:	He's upset because there was a photograph of me and Vincent	**S turns to Z**
H:	She was waiting for them	**H turns to Z**
Z:	. . . . Jealous are you, Harry?	**Z × bottom DSL**

Notice in this a number of points. Harry and Sandra turn in different directions – always keeping their faces to the audience. Sightlines clear. The questions 1 and 2 are answered:

1. Apart: Reason? the stage distance between them helps show the emotional distance.
2. Sandra: Reason? Zigger sidles up to her and so isolates Harry.

The answer to 3 should be clear: Sandra and Zigger will exit USR; Harry from another exit.

It is very important to *stress* that with **blocking** there is no right or wrong answer: the suggestions made for scene 35 are *only* suggestions. There are almost certainly other ways of blocking this scene. But good blocking will always have a reason(s) for it – finding the centre of attention, providing a clear view, enabling free movement.

Find a space. Use string or some marker to divide the area into the nine stage sections. Then one person calls out the movements of others in the class. Change the caller. Aim to familiarise yourself with the stage terms.

How would you block scene 35? Form into groups of four (some can be three). Each person independently block the positions and movements of Harry, Sandra and Les. When you have done this, find a space and each in turn direct the others through the movements. Whose version is the best? Why? Discuss the group's **ideal** blocking for the scene.

Read through scene 17. Here Harry is torn between Zigger and Les. Block the movements of the actors. You may work in a small group and experiment practically before putting your ideas on paper.

At the end of the scene the Chorus sings. Peter Terson had the chorus permanently positioned Upstage in the first production of **Zigger Zagger**. Would you? Where would you locate them?

The Big Match

The language of **Zigger Zagger** may be thought by some as offensive. Others will see it as an attempt to communicate the reality of modern problems. If one is prepared to risk the language, **Zigger Zagger** is an ideal school play. Why?

1 A large cast and thus many involved. No one 'hogs' the limelight.
2 Scope for female parts: Mrs Philton, Edna, Sandra, Glenice, 1st and 2nd Girl on the bus, and also parts like teacher, dentist, student, letter reader, etc.
3 Many skills necessary: dramatic, artistic, practical, and musical.

To stage **Zigger Zagger** requires co-operation – something Zigger himself would never learn!

The director has a number of important jobs. Here are some of them:

Casting

Who in your class is going to play Zigger, Harry, Sandra, Edna, Les, the Bus Conductor, the Vicar, etc?

Make a chart

Give everybody in your class a part. Be sure to give reasons for your choices. Compare and discuss your choices.

Character's name	Physical appearance	Voice	Personality / character	Person in class best suited	Reasons
Zigger	white male tall (?) hard bright insolent eyes, punk haircut (?) scar (?) tattoo (?)	loud, deep, and aggresive accent (?)	fanatical, violent, threatening	Brian Smith	?
Harry	?	?	?	?	?

Rehearsal Schedules

The director mustn't waste time. Rehearsals must be planned. The Chorus is in most scenes, but it would be silly to expect them to turn up for every rehearsal. Probably the director will deal with them separately. Only near the performance dates will they rehearse with the cast.

The director studies the play and groups certain scenes together. These will be scenes where the same characters appear.

The first scene has only Zigger and Harry. Are there any others like this?

Scene 10	Zigger & Harry
Scene 13	Zigger & Harry & Les
Scene 17	Zigger & Harry & Les
Scene 18	Harry
Scene 27	Zigger & Harry & Sandra
Scene 29	Harry & Sandra
Scene 32	Harry & Sandra
Scene 35	Zigger & Harry & Sandra

Some scenes are short, some are not. A typical rehearsal might take, say, three scenes: 1, 10, 18. This would involve calling two people. No one is left hanging around, waiting. What happens, instead, if the rehearsal is for scenes 1, 2, 3?

Go through the play, listing the characters in each scene. Work out a timetable for rehearsals – try to link 'similar' scenes.

Publicity

To attract an audience a play needs a good poster. The director will need to approve the design:

Here is the poster advertising **Zigger Zagger**.

Now design your poster for your production of **Zigger Zagger**. Make it eye-catching. Don't forget necessary information!

Productions also require tickets and programmes. The programme usually gives credits for directing, acting, lighting, staging, stage-managing, sound, costume, make-up, refreshments, and anyone who helps in any way! Also, sometimes, it contains local advertising. Design your tickets and programme.

Lastly, your school production must be recorded. Video is best but not always possible. Write an account for your school magazine.